PRIMARY SOURCE DETECTIVES

WHO TRAVELED TO THE MOON?

D0175949

Neil Morris

Chicago, Illinois

© 2014 Heinemann Library
an imprint of Capstone Global Library, LLC
Chicago, Illinois

To contact Capstone Global Library, please
call 800-747-4992, or visit our web site
www.capstonepub.com

Edited by Andrew Farrow, Patrick Catel, and
  Vaarunika Dharmapala
Designed by Steve Mead
Original illustrations © Capstone Global
  Library Ltd 2014
Illustrated by HL Studios
Picture research by Ruth Blair
Originated by Capstone Global Library Ltd
Printed in China

17 16 15 14 13
10 9 8 7 6 5 4 3 2 1

**Library of Congress Cataloging-in-
Publication Data**
Morris, Neil, 1946- author.
  Who traveled to the moon? / Neil Morris.
    pages cm.—(Primary source detectives)
  Includes bibliographical references and
index.
  ISBN 978-1-4329-9605-5 (hb)—ISBN 978-1-
4329-9612-3 (pb) 1. Project Apollo (U.S.)—
History—Juvenile literature. 2. Astronauts—
United States—History—Juvenile literature.
3. Project Apollo (U.S.)—History—Sources—
Juvenile literature. 4. Astronauts—United
States—History—Sources—Juvenile
literature. 5. Moon—Exploration—History—
Juvenile literature. 6. Space flight to the
moon—History—Juvenile literature. I. Title.

  TL789.8.U6A5563 2014
  629.45'40922—dc23
2013015847

Acknowledgments
We would like to thank the following for
permission to reproduce photographs:
Corbis pp. 35 (© Eric Robert/Sygma), 47;
Getty Images pp. 11, 12, 27 & 40 (Time &
Life Pictures), 14 (SSPL), 17 (Mondadori),
25 (NASA/Handout), 45, 50 (Apic/Hulton
Archive); NASA pp. 4, 7, 9, 28, 29, 30, 37, 38,
43, 46, 48, 52, 53, 56; Science Photo Library
pp. 20, 22, 44 & 54 (NASA); Superstock pp.
19 (JTB Photo), 33 (Science and Society).

Cover photograph of *Apollo 11* engaged
in extravehicular activity reproduced with
permission of NASA (Glenn Research
Center).

Page 51: From A MAN ON THE MOON
by Andrew Chaikin, copyright (c) 1994 by
Andrew Chaikin. Used by permission of
Viking Penguin, a division of Penguin Group
(USA) LLC.

CONTENTS

"THE *EAGLE* HAS LANDED"...4

WHO WERE THE FIRST MEN ON THE MOON? 6

HOW DID THE ASTRONAUTS GET THERE? 14

REACHING THE MOON 20

WHO WERE THE OTHER LUNAR
ASTRONAUTS?...30

WHO TRAINED TO GO TO THE MOON?..................40

WHAT DID THE LUNAR
ASTRONAUTS ACHIEVE?..48

TIMELINE 58

GLOSSARY..60

FIND OUT MORE 62

INDEX..64

Some words are shown in bold, **like this**. You can find out what they mean by looking in the glossary.

"THE *EAGLE* HAS LANDED"

On July 20, 1969, just after 3 o'clock in the afternoon based on the clocks in **Mission Control** on Earth, a small spacecraft approached the surface of the Moon. The spacecraft was a **lunar module (LM)** code-named *Eagle*. In it were two astronauts, whose aim was to become the first humans ever to walk on the Moon. The commander of the mission, Neil Armstrong, heard Mission Control in Houston, Texas, announce "30 seconds." He and the module pilot, Buzz Aldrin, knew this referred to the time left until their fuel ran out. They needed to touch down, and they needed to do so very soon. Nine seconds later, a contact light came on in the spacecraft. Then, after another 18 seconds, Armstrong spoke the words that everyone involved in the *Apollo 11* program had been longing to hear: "Houston, Tranquility Base here. The *Eagle* has landed."

▼ This photograph of the *Eagle* was taken from the *Apollo 11* **command module (CM)**.

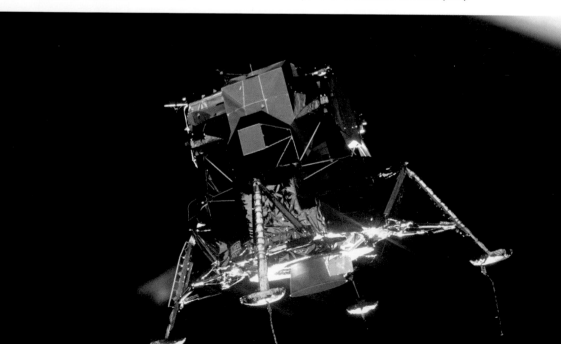

WORLDWIDE AUDIENCE

As the first humans landed on the Moon, around 600 million people watched the event live on television. Viewers knew they were watching history being made. But many details of the first Moon landing, and the events leading up to it, were not known to viewers at the time. For example, they were not aware of the significance of the number 30 or the small amount of fuel left in the lunar module. However, the U.S. space agency kept records of the event, so people who were interested in these facts could check them out later. (See page 21 for more information about the low fuel problem.)

A DECADE'S WORK

Just over eight years earlier, on May 25, 1961, President John F. Kennedy had announced that the United States aimed to land a man on the Moon and return him safely to Earth "before this decade is out." "No single space project in this period will be more impressive to mankind," the president said. When the *Apollo 11* astronauts landed safely back on Earth, four days after landing on the Moon, it meant that the goal had been achieved, with five months to spare. It was an extraordinary achievement, and many books, newspaper articles, and documentary films have been written and made about this and the other lunar landings.

MOONWALKERS

This is the story of 12 men who walked on the Moon. Their amazing achievements took place between July 1969 and December 1972, and no one has set foot on the Moon since. Another 12 American astronauts traveled to the Moon without landing on it, and many thousands of other people helped make the lunar missions happen. In this book, we will look carefully at how we know so much about the missions, and how you can find out more. There are many records, and people have done a great deal of research on the subject. You will also discover how you can add your own research to the list.

WHO WERE THE FIRST MEN ON THE MOON?

The first men on the Moon were the commander and lunar pilot of the *Apollo 11* mission, Neil Armstrong and Buzz Aldrin. A third astronaut, Michael Collins, went with them. He flew around the Moon as pilot of the command module, while his two colleagues took the lunar module down to the surface.

There are many research sources for the story of *Apollo 11*—more than for any other space mission. The three astronauts have taken part in many interviews and even written their own books. There are also numerous official sources, including countless documents published by NASA (the U.S. National Aeronautics and Space Administration), which was responsible for the mission. NASA's web site is a great place to start your research about *Apollo 11* or any other U.S. space mission (see page 23).

HISTORY DETECTIVES:
WHAT EXACTLY IS RESEARCH?

The word *research* comes from the French *rechercher*, and it means to "discover facts by investigating systematically." When you research a subject, you investigate it in detail by studying sources carefully. The sources allow you to study evidence and establish the facts. Your research means that you can reach conclusions about the subject you are investigating. Research into the question "Who went to the Moon?" will tell you more than just facts about 12 astronauts. It will answer questions about how they got there, why they went, and what exactly they did on the Moon.

⚠ This shows the *Apollo 11* crew, from left to right: Neil Armstrong (the first man on the Moon), Michael Collins (pilot of the command module), and Buzz Aldrin (second man on the Moon).

WHO IN HISTORY

NEIL ALDEN ARMSTRONG
1930–2012

BORN: Wapakoneta, Ohio

EDUCATION: Bachelor's degree in **aeronautical engineering**, Purdue University, 1955; master's degree in Aerospace Engineering, University of Southern California, 1970

EXPERIENCE: As a pilot in the U.S. Navy, Armstrong flew 78 missions in the Korean War (1950–1953). From 1955 to 1971, he worked for NASA. He later taught for several years.

NASA EXPERIENCE: Initially a test pilot on high-speed aircraft, in 1962 Neil began astronaut training in Group 2 (pilot astronauts). He was command pilot on the 1966 *Gemini 8* mission, the first successful **docking** of two spacecraft. He commanded *Apollo 11*, the first manned lunar landing mission. He was later responsible for aeronautic research and technology.

TIME IN SPACE: 206 hours and 12 minutes; 2 hours and 32 minutes on the Moon

START OF THE ASTRONAUTS' ADVENTURE

On January 6, 1969, NASA's director of flight crew operations, Deke Slayton, called Neil Armstrong into his office. Slayton told Armstrong that he would be commander of *Apollo 11*, which was scheduled to take off for the Moon six months later. He also told him that the other crew members would be Buzz Aldrin and Michael Collins. Slayton said that if all went well with Apollo missions 9 and 10, scheduled for launch in March and May, *Apollo 11* would aim for the first lunar landing in July.

TRAINING FOR MOON LANDING

In the spring of 1969, the three astronauts chosen for *Apollo 11* spent a great deal of time training for the first lunar mission. Much time was spent learning to fly the lunar module, which was seen as the most difficult and

WHO IN HISTORY

EDWIN EUGENE "BUZZ" ALDRIN, JR.
BORN: 1930 in Montclair, New Jersey

EDUCATION: Bachelor's degree in mechanical engineering, U.S. Military Academy at West Point, 1951; PhD in **astronautics**, Massachusetts Institute of Technology, 1963

EXPERIENCE: As a U.S. Air Force fighter pilot, he flew 66 combat missions in the Korean War. He became an aerial gunnery instructor, then aide to the dean of faculty at the Air Force Academy. He was a flight commander in Germany, then worked at the Gemini Target Office of the Air Force Space Systems Division, Los Angeles. From 1963 to 1971, he worked for NASA. He was later commandant of the Aerospace Research Pilot's School, a consultant for Comprehensive Care Corporation, and lectured and consulted on space sciences with Starcraft Enterprises.

NASA EXPERIENCE: He was a member of Group 3, 1963. As pilot of *Gemini 12*, in 1966, he set a new record for **extravehicular activity** (EVA), spending 5½ hours outside the spacecraft. Aldrin was lunar module pilot of *Apollo 11*.

TIME IN SPACE: 289 hours and 53 minutes; 2 hours and 15 minutes on the Moon

dangerous part of the mission. The crew practiced the descent to the lunar surface in a **flight simulator**. This was an exact copy of the real spacecraft, with the same dials and controls. It rotated and tilted just like the real thing and even showed lunar views through the windows.

There was also a machine called a Lunar Landing Research Vehicle, nicknamed the "flying bedstead" by the astronauts. It was very difficult to fly, but then so was the lunar module. Just a year before, Neil Armstrong had been practicing in a "bedstead" when it went out of control. He **ejected** safely, and the vehicle crashed. Despite this, Armstrong insisted on practicing and flying the machine again in spring 1969.

▲ The first "flying bedstead" took off in 1964 at NASA's Flight Research Center in California. A test pilot was at the controls.

WHY "BUZZ"?

In many documents, you will find the *Apollo 11* lunar pilot named as Edwin rather than Buzz Aldrin. His nickname, "Buzz," came about because of his sister Fay Ann. As a child, she called him "buzzer" rather than "brother." Edwin liked the nickname "Buzz" so much that in 1979 he officially changed his name.

MICHAEL COLLINS
BORN: October 31, 1930, in Rome, Italy

EDUCATION: Bachelor's degree, U.S. Military Academy at West Point, 1952

EXPERIENCE: Formerly a U.S. Air Force fighter pilot and experimental flight test officer, Collins worked for NASA from 1963 to 1970. He became assistant secretary of state for Public Affairs, then director of the National Air and Space Museum, Washington, D.C. He retired from the Air Force with the rank of major general. Later, he was vice president of field operations for the Vought Corporation, before forming the Michael Collins Associates consulting firm in Washington, D.C.

NASA EXPERIENCE: A member of Group 3, 1963, he was backup pilot for *Gemini 7* in 1965, pilot of *Gemini 10* in 1966, and command module pilot of *Apollo 11*.

TIME IN SPACE: 266 hours and 4 minutes

FLYING BACKGROUND

The biographies of the three *Apollo 11* astronauts show that they all had a military background as fighter pilots. Neil Armstrong left the U.S. Navy in 1952 and three years later became a test pilot on high-speed aircraft, working first for the Aeronautics Committee that later became NASA. He flew more than 200 different types of aircraft, including rockets and helicopters. In 1962, he applied to become a member of the second group of astronauts to be trained (see page 41 for a list of these groups). In fact, his application arrived a week after the deadline, but a former test pilot colleague slipped the application into the right folder just in time for him to be considered.

MILITARY MEN

Buzz Aldrin and Michael Collins were U.S. Air Force pilots. Aldrin's first application to become an astronaut was rejected because he had never been a test pilot. In 1963, the rules were changed, Aldrin re-applied, and he was accepted into the third group of astronauts. He was the first astronaut with a PhD (an advanced degree) and became known as

"Dr. Rendezvous." This was because he was an expert at docking spacecraft together (*rendezvous* means to meet at an agreed upon place). Michael Collins had the necessary qualifications as a test pilot, but his application for Group 2 was nevertheless rejected. Like Aldrin, he applied for Group 3 and was successful.

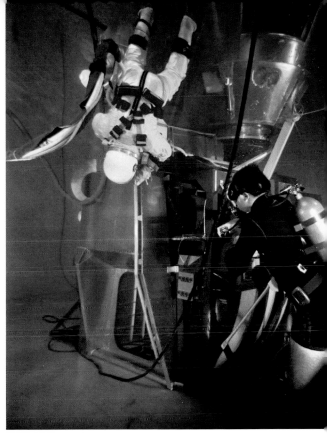

The *Apollo 11* astronauts also did underwater training, which allowed them to become used to the low **gravity** they would encounter on the Moon ▷

HISTORY DETECTIVES:
WHAT IS A PRIMARY SOURCE?

Researchers look for evidence to help them answer questions. The places where they find the evidence are called sources. Historians first look for primary sources. These are original documents that come from the period being studied and were created by people who were there at the time.

Primary sources are often written documents, such as official records, but they may also be video or audio recordings, as with the Moon landings. Diaries, letters, research papers, photographs, and interviews are also primary sources. They all record facts and events rather than interpret them.

TRAINING AND EXPERIENCE

The three *Apollo 11* astronauts were given extensive training in all aspects of space flight. They also all had experience in space before their journey together in July 1969. They had each been in space on the **Gemini** missions that led up to the Apollo program, though they had not flown together before.

BACKUP CREW

Every space mission has a backup crew, in case an astronaut gets sick or has to drop out for any other reason. For *Apollo 11*, the backups were:

- Jim Lovell (commander), who was also backup pilot for *Gemini 4*, pilot of *Gemini 7,* backup command pilot for Gemini 9, command pilot of *Gemini 12*, command module pilot of *Apollo 8*, and commander of *Apollo 13*.
- Bill Anders (command module pilot), who was also backup pilot for *Gemini 11* and lunar module pilot of *Apollo 8*.
- Fred Haise (lunar module pilot), who was also backup lunar module pilot for *Apollo 8*, lunar module pilot of *Apollo 13*, and backup commander for *Apollo 16*.

▼ The *Apollo 11* astronauts relax and talk during some time off from their training (from left to right: Neil Armstrong, Michael Collins, and Buzz Aldrin).

Lovell and Anders flew to a distance of about 68 miles (110 kilometers) above the Moon's surface with *Apollo 8*. Lovell was originally a backup for *Apollo 8* and replaced Michael Collins when he needed a surgical operation. Lovell and Haise also went close to the Moon with *Apollo 13* (see page 32). None of these three astronauts landed on the Moon.

THE RIGHT STUFF?

In 1979, Tom Wolfe wrote a book about test pilots and early astronauts called *The Right Stuff*. He thought astronauts had to have special high-level qualities—what he called "the right stuff." One of the aims of the early space program was to learn about how the human body reacts to space travel. The lunar astronauts had to be fit and physically able to meet all sorts of unknown challenges. Of course, all the other astronauts before and after them also had to have these qualities, including the backup crews.

They also had to make sure they stayed healthy. On July 5, 1969, just 11 days before launch, the *Apollo 11* astronauts were asked to give interviews to the press. They turned up wearing hospital masks and then took their places inside a plastic booth. Was it a joke? No: they had to be in **quarantine** for three weeks before launch, to avoid getting sick.

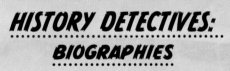

HISTORY DETECTIVES:
BIOGRAPHIES

A biography is an account of someone's life. Biographies of the lunar astronauts, along with others involved in the lunar program, are central to research on finding out who went to the Moon.

There is a list of NASA astronaut biographies, along with international astronauts and cosmonauts, at www.jsc. nasa.gov/Bios/index.html.

HOW DID THE ASTRONAUTS GET THERE?

The *Apollo 11* astronauts traveled to the Moon using a system of space travel called **lunar-orbit rendezvous**. A powerful *Saturn V* rocket launched a spacecraft with three astronauts into space. The spacecraft was made up of three modules. The cone-shaped command module (CM) was the control center and contained the astronauts. For most of the mission, it was joined to the **service module (SM)**, which carried fuel, oxygen, water, and a power system. The lunar module (LM) carried two astronauts from the CM to the Moon, while the third astronaut orbited the Moon in the joined **command/service module (CSM)**.

▼ The *Saturn V* rocket for *Apollo 11* travels on a mobile platform to its launchpad at the Kennedy Space Center in Florida.

MOON MISSION TIMES

When you read about the Apollo missions, you might get confused about times. Many sources refer to the time in Houston, Texas, where Mission Control was based. By this logic, *Apollo 11* lifted off at 8:32 a.m. The local time at the Kennedy Space Center in Florida (EDT, Eastern Daylight Time) was 1 hour later, 9:32 a.m. The official NASA timeline shows events in GMT (Greenwich Mean Time) or UT (Universal Time), both making launch time 13:32. It also shows GET (Ground Elapsed Time), or mission time, in hours, minutes, and seconds, timing launch at 000:00:00.00. For comparison, touchdown on the Moon on July 20 was at:

3:17 p.m. (or 15:17) Houston time
4:17 p.m. (or 16:17) Space Center/Florida time
8:17 p.m. (or 20:17) Greenwich Mean Time (GMT)
102:45:39.9 mission time.

In the description of the *Apollo 11* mission in this book, we generally use Houston time.

The moonwalkers returned to orbit in part of the lunar module, where they joined up with the CSM. They transferred into the CSM before traveling back to Earth. Finally, the CM separated as it approached Earth, before splashing down in the ocean. You can follow this journey for *Apollo 11* and ask many research questions along the way.

BLASTOFF!

At 8:00 a.m. Houston time, 9:00 a.m. local time, on July 16, 1969, the countdown showed that there were just 32 minutes to blastoff. The three astronauts were in the spacecraft at the top of the *Saturn V* rocket, making final checks with Mission Control. As the huge rocket blasted off, TV viewers heard a voice in Mission Control say, "We have a liftoff." Just 2 minutes and 42 seconds later, the stage-one rockets had finished their takeoff job and fell away to Earth. The spacecraft orbited Earth one and a half times and then was ready to head toward the Moon. First, there was the complicated procedure of separating the CM from the module housing the LM, turning around, and docking again. Once this was done, the astronauts had their first meal—chicken salad, apple sauce, and shrimp cocktail. Then they settled down for the three-day journey to the Moon.

HEAVY-LIFT VEHICLE

The rocket used for all six Apollo missions was a *Saturn V*. According to NASA, this heavy-lift vehicle, as they call it, "was the most powerful rocket that had ever flown successfully." The statistics on the next page show how enormous and powerful the *Saturn V* was. There are many books and web sites about the rocket's technical details, which you could use for research. At the same time, you could look for ways for nonspecialists to understand the figures. For example, according to the NASA web site section on **rocketry**, *Saturn V*:

- generated more power at launch than 85 Hoover Dams
- used as much fuel on one mission as a car driving around the world 800 times
- launched the weight of 10 school buses into space.

ROCKET STAGES

Each of the three stages of *Saturn V* burned its engines until it was out of fuel, then fell away. The first stage had five engines for liftoff, which burned for 2½ minutes and blasted the rocket to an altitude of about 42 miles (68 kilometers). The second stage burned for 6 minutes and took it almost into Earth's orbit. The third stage had two burns, totaling more than 8 minutes, and sent the spacecraft into orbit and then toward the Moon. According to NASA, "The first two stages fell into the ocean after separation. The third stage either stayed in space or hit the moon." This would make a good research project. Did NASA recover any of these parts? Where are they now? Start by looking at NASA's web page on a restored *Saturn V*: www.nasa.gov/centers/johnson/home/jsc_grand_opening.html.

SATURN V
STATISTICS

Number of rocket stages: 3

Height: 363 feet (111 meters)

Diameter: 33 feet (10 meters)

Mass at liftoff: 6,262,500 pounds (2,840,622 kilograms)

Thrust: 7.6 million pounds (34.5 million newtons)

Payload to orbit: 285,000 pounds (129,300 kilograms)

Payload to Moon: 107,000 pounds (48,500 kilograms)

Propellants: kerosene, liquid oxygen, liquid hydrogen

DETECTIVE WORK BENEATH THE OCEAN

The American businessman Jeff Bezos, who founded the online retailer Amazon, has a passion for spaceflight history. The quotations in the box below are from his web site. He funded a team of deep-sea explorers to search for the engines that lifted *Apollo 11* into space, somewhere in the Atlantic Ocean off Florida. A year later, he reported that he had recovered two engines and says that he will ask NASA, which owns the engines, to put them on display at the Smithsonian National Air and Space Museum in Washington, D.C., or the Museum of Flight in Seattle.

This is an amazing piece of physical research, which historians might put under the heading of **industrial archaeology** (the study of past industrial equipment and buildings). This story shows how new information and advances in technology can tell us more about the past even as we move further away in time.

F–1 ENGINE RECOVERY

March 28, 2012

On July 16, 1969, the world watched as five particular F-1 engines fired in concert, beginning the historic Apollo 11 *mission. Those five F-1s burned for just a few minutes, and then plunged back to Earth into the Atlantic Ocean, just as NASA planned… A year or so ago, I started to wonder, with the right team of undersea pros, could we find and potentially recover the F-1 engines that started mankind's mission to the moon? I'm excited to report that, using* state-of-the-art deep sea **sonar***, the team has found the* Apollo 11 *engines lying 14,000 feet [4,267 meters] below the surface, and we're making plans to attempt to raise one or more of them from the ocean floor.*

March 20, 2013

We've seen an underwater wonderland—an incredible sculpture garden of twisted F-1 engines that tells the story of a fiery and violent end, one that serves testament to the Apollo program. We…have now recovered many prime pieces… We're bringing home enough major components to fashion displays of two flown F-1 engines.

Sincerely,

Jeff Bezos

bezosexpeditions.com

▲ This restored *Saturn V* rocket is on display at the Space Center Houston in Texas. Each of its five engines measures 12.2 feet (3.7 meters) across.

HISTORY DETECTIVES:
SEARCHING THE INTERNET

A good way to explore the Internet is to use a search engine. It can do a lot of work for you, but only if you use the search sensibly. If you type "who went to the moon" into a search engine such as Google, you get hundreds of millions of results. The exact number changes all the time, as search engines search the web constantly. Each entry usually quotes a couple of sentences containing the searched text. These entries might not all be relevant to your search, because the search engine is only giving you a list of sites with your words in it. Take a look at the likely web sites, and you may find links from them to other useful sites. Of course, the search engine is just the beginning of your research. It is a tool to get you started. It cannot possibly complete your research by itself.

REACHING THE MOON

At 12:22 p.m. on July 19, 1969, the *Apollo 11* spacecraft reached the Moon and went into **lunar orbit**. The following day, at 1:12 p.m., the lunar module separated from the command module. Neil Armstrong and Buzz Aldrin began their 60-mile (96-kilometer) descent to the Moon. By 3:04 p.m., the LM was 50,000 feet (15,000 meters) above the surface, but just two minutes later, an alarm sounded in the LM. No one was sure exactly what was wrong, but Mission Control decided that it was possible to continue with the landing. When the LM was just 2,953 feet (900 meters) above the surface, an alarm sounded again, but then stopped. *Eagle* flew on, low on fuel, and landed at 3:17 and 39 seconds p.m., nearly 103 hours after taking off from Earth. Armstrong and Aldrin were the first men on the Moon.

▼ Four teams of flight controllers worked in shifts at Mission Control in Houston. They used computers, monitors, maps, and TV screens.

HOW LOW WAS *EAGLE'S* FUEL?

A useful source of information is NASA's Lunar Surface Journal (see the box below). According to the journal, *Apollo 11* astronauts received a "countdown to a 'Bingo' fuel call which meant 'land in 20 seconds or **abort**,'" which would have meant returning to the command module. So the "30 seconds" mentioned on page 4 of this book meant "until the Bingo call," not until they ran out of fuel completely. In the technical debrief after the mission in 1969, Armstrong said, "We were close to running out of fuel. We were hitting our abort limit… I guess that, at that altitude, running out of fuel wasn't a consideration. Because we would have let it just quit on us, probably, and let it fall on in." So he was confident that from their height at 30 seconds (less than 20 feet, or 6.1 meters), *Eagle* could have dropped safely on to the lunar surface. In an interview in 2001, Armstrong added, "I was perhaps probably less concerned about it than a lot of people watching down here on Earth."

So, how did Armstrong and Aldrin get home, if there was no fuel left? The lunar module had a **descent stage** and an **ascent stage**, each with its own fuel supply. Only the descent stage's fuel was used for landing. To leave the Moon, the engine of the smaller ascent stage was used. The descent stage was left on the Moon. Many researchers have investigated how much fuel remained. Their figures range from about 15 seconds to NASA's later calculation that 45 seconds was left.

LUNAR SURFACE JOURNAL

The Lunar Surface Journal is "a record of the lunar surface operations conducted by the six pairs of astronauts who landed on the Moon…intended as a resource for anyone wanting to know what happened during the missions and why. It includes a corrected transcript of all recorded conversations between the lunar surface crews and Houston." You will find the Apollo Lunar Surface Journal at www.hq.nasa.gov/alsj.

HISTORY DETECTIVES: SECONDARY SOURCES

Secondary sources discuss and interpret events. They are often written or made later than the period in question. Secondary sources include books, articles, and web pages; these may also quote or refer to primary sources. They will help you make up your mind about questions you are investigating. Your research will still be original, because it will be slightly different than everyone else's.

▼ The TV camera on the *Eagle* photographed Armstrong (left) and Aldrin planting the U.S. flag.

MOONWALKING

After landing, the astronauts were supposed to rest, but they found this impossible. They asked to be allowed to leave the LM earlier than planned, and at 7:21 p.m. began to put on their spacesuits. At 9:28 p.m., they tried to open the LM's door, but it was stuck. At last, Aldrin pulled back part of the door's seal and it opened. At the top of the ladder leading down to the Moon's surface, Armstrong pulled a cord, and a small TV camera popped out of the side of the LM. Armstrong stepped onto the Moon's surface at 9:56 p.m., and Aldrin joined him there 19 minutes later. They planted the U.S. flag, then began collecting soil and rock samples. They also took a telephone call from President Richard Nixon (see the box at right). The astronauts set up scientific instruments, such as a **seismometer** to measure **moonquakes**, and a reflector for laser beams, which allowed scientists to measure the exact distance to the Moon for the very first time.

PRESIDENT NIXON'S PHONE CALL

"Hello, Neil and Buzz, I'm talking to you by telephone from the Oval Room at the White House, and this certainly has to be the most historic telephone call ever made. I just can't tell you how proud we all are of what you have achieved... Because of what you have done, the heavens have become a part of man's world."

HISTORY DETECTIVES: NAVIGATING NASA

The best web site for researching our topic is www.nasa.gov. At the home page, you could choose the section "For students." From the drop-down menu in the "Missions" section, select "All missions," then "Apollo." There you will find videos, images, **interactive** features, drawings, and articles. There is also a box of "Related sites," one of which is "NASA History Office," where you can find out more about the Apollo missions. **Hyperlinks** are highlighted and become underlined when you move your cursor over them. You can then click to go straight to that information.

ONE SMALL STEP FOR [A] MAN

A web site called the Phrase Finder lists Neil Armstrong's words upon setting foot on the Moon as "a strong contender as the most famous line ever to have been uttered." But what did he actually say? Researchers have been debating this ever since. On television the world heard, "That's one small step for man, one giant leap for mankind." After the mission, Armstrong said he meant to say "one small step for *a* man," meaning a small step for one individual and a giant leap for the whole of humankind. Without the *a*, his words really mean "a small step for humankind but a giant leap for humankind," which does not make sense. Asked in 1971 if the *a* had been lost in transmission, Armstrong replied, "We'll never know."

The editor of the Lunar Surface Journal, Eric Jones, listened repeatedly to the recording without hearing any evidence of an *a*. But in 2006, Peter Ford, a computer programer, claimed to have found the missing *a* in the **waveform** of the audio file, meaning that the word was spoken but not transmitted or recorded. Neil Armstrong's response was, "I find his conclusion persuasive." Other audio experts disagree.

You could do your own research on the Internet. Put the famous words into a search engine to start. After your research, draw your own conclusion.

THE APOLLO GUIDANCE COMPUTER

Another interesting area for research is the computer that helped get men to the Moon. In the 1960s and 1970s, computers took up enormous amounts of space, and by today's standards, their "power" seems weak. Apollo spacecraft used a mini computer that was fitted to the command module and the lunar module. Astronauts communicated with either computer using a display and keyboard unit (DSKY, pronounced "disky"). To make a command, they keyed in two double-digit numbers, called verbs and nouns. For example, keying in Verb 16, Noun 68 told the computer to display the lunar module's altitude, speed, and distance to the landing site. According to a web site called Computer Weekly, the Apollo computer was "no more powerful than a pocket calculator." It had about 64 **kilobytes** of memory. Compare this with an iPhone, which has at least 16 **gigabytes** (or 16 million kilobytes).

BACK TO THE COMMAND MODULE

Just after midnight, Armstrong followed Aldrin back into the LM. They had been moonwalking for 1¾ hours and had a lot of work to do to get ready for *Eagle*'s takeoff. The countdown finally began 12 hours later, and *Eagle* took off smoothly at 12:54 p.m. on July 21. In the LM *Columbia*, Michael Collins took photographs of the approaching *Eagle*. The LM docked safely at 4:34 p.m., and the three astronauts were reunited. Seven hours later, the spacecraft left lunar orbit and headed back to Earth.

▼ The *Apollo 11* lunar module returns to the command module after the successful landing. CM pilot Michael Collins took the photograph. In the background, we see Earth in the darkness of space above the Moon's surface.

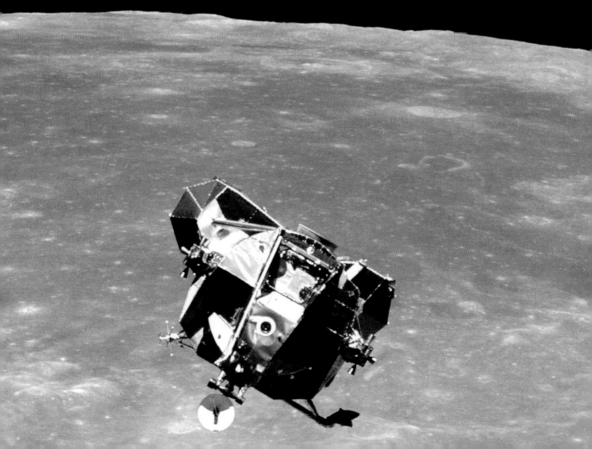

SEARCHING FOR MISSING TAPES

Even in the modern age, valuable sources sometimes go missing. In 2006, National Public Radio (NPR) reported that the original videotapes showing the *Apollo 11* astronauts on the Moon were missing. Converted tapes still existed, but historians were interested in the originals, which modern technology could clean up to give better images.

For three years, researchers looked through logbooks and other handwritten records, hoping to find out what had happened to the tapes. At last, they came to the conclusion that NASA had erased the originals in the 1970s to reuse them on satellite missions. But there was still hope. Old documents revealed that the lunar camera's signals had also been recorded on 2-inch (5-centimeter) tapes at the Applied Physics Laboratory near Baltimore, Maryland. There was another huge search, but again nothing was found. In 2009, on the 40th anniversary of *Apollo 11*, NASA had the converted videotapes restored. You can see them in high definition at www.nasa.gov/multimedia/hd/apollo11.html.

Think About This

Human interest stories

"Human interest" is the aspect of a story that readers enjoy because it describes the experiences and emotions of the people involved. This might include background research into the astronauts' families, friends, colleagues, and others. In his book *A Man on the Moon*, author Andrew Chaikin describes the feelings of the *Apollo 11* astronauts' wives—Joan Aldrin, Janet Armstrong, and Pat Collins—during the mission. This offers more information on the issue of low fuel, as Joan Aldrin watched the landing on TV:

> *Buzz had always said that the moment of truth would be the lift-off from the moon, but in her [Joan's] mind it was the landing… The* Eagle *was very low, and she could barely stand the tension. Rusty told her that the fuel was now down to a matter of seconds, and that Neil and Buzz had not yet found a place to land… Finally, in the midst of the numbers, she heard Buzz say, "Okay, engine stop." Those words she understood: they had made it.*

DETECTIVE WORK

In an article on the web site of the Amateur Astronomers Association of New York (aaa.org/node/458), John Delaney writes that he read an account of the landing in the *New York Times* by reporter John Noble Wilford. This stated that around 3 a.m. on July 21, 1969, Wilford gazed up at the full Moon and wondered how the lunar astronauts might be feeling. Yet Delaney remembered reading that the mission was planned so that the Sun was low on the lunar horizon and the temperature not too high. Surely that meant that the Moon was not full on that date? His research led him to the Farmer's Almanac for July 20, 1969, where he found that the **waxing crescent Moon** set (or became invisible) before midnight. This evidence showed that Wilford had mixed up some details. Delaney writes: "Wilford's Moon observation is a minor [incorrect] detail in his masterful account of a defining moment," but Delaney wanted to use his detective work to set the astronomical record straight.

▼ Joan Aldrin looks at a picture of her husband and his fellow astronauts under the newspaper headline "*Apollo* Reaches the Moon."

RETURN AND SPLASHDOWN

At 11:35 a.m. on July 24, the *Apollo 11* spacecraft glowed with heat as it entered Earth's atmosphere. Nine minutes later, parachutes opened to slow the craft's descent toward the Pacific Ocean. It splashed down in the ocean at 11:50 a.m., and an hour later the crew members were all safely aboard the recovery ship, USS *Hornet*. On the ship, the astronauts had to go immediately into a quarantine capsule. They were kept in quarantine for three weeks before they could be reunited with their families. When that period was over, Armstrong, Aldrin, and Collins soon discovered that they were celebrities and had become heroes around the world.

CLASSIFIED INFORMATION

During the period of the Apollo program, some information must have been secret and available to authorized people only. This was the time of the "space race" between the world's two most powerful nations, the United States and the Soviet Union. The political hostility between the two countries was known as the Cold War. Therefore, it is not surprising that researchers discovered some pieces of information about the Moon landings many years later. One example is the change of location for splashdown in the Pacific Ocean at the end of the *Apollo 11* mission. The Apollo Flight Journal says that 14 hours before splashdown, Mission Control said to Michael Collins, "The weather is clobbering in at our targeted landing point due to scattered thunderstorms. We don't want to tangle with one of those, so we're going to move you."

▼ After splashdown, about 930 miles (1,500 kilometers) southwest of Hawaii, the astronauts waited to be picked up by helicopter. The fourth man is a helper from the U.S. Navy.

▲ President Nixon spoke to the astronauts in the Mobile Quarantine Facility (MQF) aboard the recovery ship. They stayed for 65 hours in the MQF, which was 35 feet (10.7 meters) long.

Twenty-six years later, in 1995, documents were declassified that allowed us to see how Mission Control found out about the bad weather. It was from **meteorologists** studying data from a spy satellite, code-named Corona, which secretly photographed areas around the Soviet Union and China. According to the weatherman with the secret information, "The [storm] would have ripped their parachutes to shreds. Without parachutes [to slow down the capsule], they'd have crashed into the ocean with a force that would have killed them instantly." He made sure that he got the information to the right people, who told Mission Control, and they changed their plans and the splashdown location.

WHO WERE THE OTHER LUNAR ASTRONAUTS?

The *Apollo 11* mission was soon followed by other successful Moon shots. In fact, five more pairs of astronauts walked on the Moon over a period of three and a half years. They all traveled to the Moon in the same way, since this had proven to be so successful. On each successive mission, the astronauts stayed on the lunar surface for longer than the previous moonwalkers did. The *Apollo 17* astronauts stayed for more than three days and walked on the Moon for nearly a day in three separate EVAs (extravehicular activities), or moonwalks. After another three-day journey back to Earth, the astronauts splashed down more than 12½ days after launch.

▼ The ninth moonwalker, John Young, salutes the U.S. flag beside the *Apollo 16* lunar module *Orion*. The photograph was taken by LM pilot Charles Duke.

MOONWALKER OVERVIEW

Here is a list of all 12 moonwalkers, in the order in which they stepped onto the Moon:

Name	Service	Age on Moon landing	Apollo mission	Date landed	Number of EVAs	Total EVA time
Neil Armstrong	NASA	38	11	July 20, 1969	1	2 hrs, 31 mins
Buzz Aldrin	U.S. Air Force	39	11	July 20, 1969	1	2 hrs, 31 mins
Pete Conrad	U.S. Navy	39	12	Nov. 19, 1969	2	7 hrs, 45 mins
Alan Bean	U.S. Navy	37	12	Nov. 19, 1969	2	7 hrs, 45 mins
Alan Shepard	U.S. Navy	47	14	Feb. 5, 1971	2	9 hrs, 21 mins
Edgar Mitchell	U.S. Navy	40	14	Feb. 5, 1971	2	9 hrs, 21 mins
David Scott	U.S. Air Force	39	15	July 30, 1971	3	18 hrs, 33 mins
James Irwin	U.S. Air Force	41	15	July 30, 1971	3	18 hrs, 33 mins
John Young	U.S. Navy	41	16	Apr. 20, 1972	3	20 hrs, 14 mins
Charles Duke	U.S. Air Force	36	16	Apr. 20, 1972	3	20 hrs, 14 mins
Eugene Cernan	U.S. Navy	38	17	Dec. 11, 1972	3	22 hrs, 2 mins
Harrison Schmitt	NASA	37	17	Dec. 11, 1972	3	22 hrs, 2 mins

WHO WENT TO THE MOON TWICE?

Three astronauts went to the Moon twice. Two of them landed on their second trip. For information about the third, Jim Lovell, see page 32.

- John Young was the first astronaut from Group 3 to go into space, with *Gemini 3*. He was scolded for smuggling a corned beef sandwich on board the spacecraft! NASA must have forgiven him, because he was CM pilot of *Apollo 10* and commander of *Apollo 16*.
- Eugene Cernan, from Group 3, was pilot of *Gemini 9A* and the third human to perform an EVA. He was LM pilot of *Apollo 10* and commander of *Apollo 17*, which makes him the only person to have flown in the LM near the Moon twice. He was the last man on the Moon, because he stepped onto the surface first but was second back into the LM.

THE OTHER LUNAR ASTRONAUTS

Here is a list of the other 12 lunar astronauts, in the order in which they went to the Moon:

Name	Service	Age on mission	Apollo mission	Date of launch
Frank Borman	U.S. Air Force	40	8	Dec. 21, 1968
Jim Lovell	U.S. Navy	40	8 13	Dec. 21, 1968 April 11, 1970
Bill Anders	U.S. Air Force	35	8	Dec. 21, 1968
Tom Stafford	U.S. Air Force	38	10	May 18, 1969
Michael Collins	U.S. Air Force	38	11	July 16, 1969
Dick Gordon	U.S. Navy	40	12	Nov. 14, 1969
Jack Swigert	NASA	38	13	April 11, 1970
Fred Haise	NASA	36	13	April 11, 1970
Stu Roosa	U.S. Air Force	37	14	Jan. 31, 1971
Al Worden	U.S. Air Force	39	15	July 26, 1971
Ken Mattingly	U.S. Navy	36	16	April 16, 1972
Ron Evans	U.S. Navy	39	17	Dec. 7, 1972

WHO WENT TWICE WITHOUT LANDING?

Jim Lovell, from Group 2, flew in space four times and went to the Moon twice. He was pilot of *Gemini 7* and commander of *Gemini 12*, with pilot Buzz Aldrin. Along with Frank Borman and Bill Anders, he was one of the first travelers to the Moon as CM pilot of *Apollo 8*, the first mission to orbit the Moon. Sixteen months later, he commanded the *Apollo 13* mission, which was very nearly a disaster (see page 34). Altogether, Lovell spent nearly 30 days in space. A crater on the far side of the Moon is named after him.

ART ON THE MOON?

Gwendolyn Wright is a professor of architecture at Columbia University, in New York. She also works as an investigative reporter for the Public Broadcasting Service (PBS). In 2010, she explored what she called "the first piece of art to land on the Moon." It had been rumored that a ceramic chip, the size of a postage stamp, was attached to a leg of the landing stage of the *Apollo 12* lunar module. On the chip were miniature artworks by six artists, including Andy Warhol. When making the program, Professor Wright spoke to one of the six artists, Forrest Myers, a launchpad foreman, and astronaut

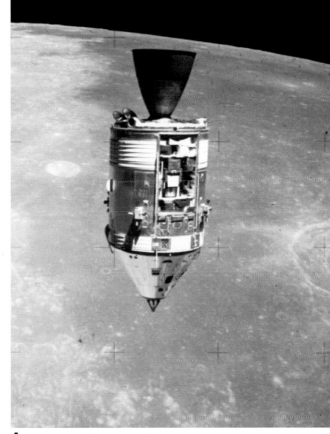

▲ The *Apollo 15* command/service module *Endeavour*, photographed from lunar module *Falcon*, orbits the Moon. The CM pilot was Al Worden (see the table on page 32), who stayed in *Endeavour* while his colleagues walked on the Moon. The CSM made 74 lunar orbits.

Alan Bean. The astronaut said that he and others took a little cloth bag, called a "personal preference kit," with them to the Moon. It seems that some of these were left on the Moon, wrapped in the gold foil used for parts of the lunar landers. But Bean knew nothing about the art chip. Professor Wright discovered that a certain "John F.," who worked on the lunar module, confirmed that the chip was in place by sending a telegram to Forrest Myers before *Apollo 12* blasted off. The program ended: "So if you were John F., or if you know someone who you think could have been John F., please let us know." At the beginning of 2013, his identity remained a mystery. You can find out more at www.pbs.org.

HISTORY DETECTIVES:
FINDING WHAT YOU WANT ON THE INTERNET

It is not easy to select trustworthy sites on the Internet. Any sites ending in .gov (short for "government") will be accurate: they are official sites of the U.S. government. Another trustworthy suffix (ending) is .edu, which stands for institutions of higher education, such as colleges.

One of the first results given by a search engine might be an article in the online encyclopedia Wikipedia. Be aware that Wikipedia is compiled and edited by members of the public, so always double check facts in another source. However, the notes and other references at the end of a Wikipedia article can lead you to some helpful resources.

Say you wanted to see the timeline for an Apollo mission, such as the second successful landing. If you search for "Apollo 12 timeline" in a major search engine, among other results, you will find two very useful but different sources. If you click on the results at history.nasa.gov, you will see a comprehensive list with 320 lines. In contrast, if you choose the article at www.lpi.usra.edu, you will see a concise timeline with 12 lines of data written by the Lunar and Planetary Institute.

NEAR DISASTER

The Apollo Moon missions did not always go according to plan. The third lunar landing mission, *Apollo 13*, had to be abandoned after an oxygen tank in the service module split and exploded. The spacecraft was then about 200,000 miles (320,000 kilometers) from Earth, more than three-quarters of the way to the Moon. The spacecraft was badly damaged, but it was decided that the safest option was to go around the Moon rather than attempt a complicated turning **maneuver**. The lunar module acted as a lifeboat, and the three-man crew used limited power ingeniously to return safely to Earth. The command module is on display at the Cosmosphere and Space Center in Hutchinson, Kansas.

In 1995, a movie was made about the mission, called *Apollo 13* and starring Tom Hanks as Jim Lovell (who went to the Moon twice; see page 32). The film was nominated for nine Academy Award (Oscars)—including one for best picture—and won two. The movie was based on information from NASA and was technically accurate, though some of the dialogue was different. For example, the most famous line in the movie is when Hanks says, "Houston, we have a problem." This has since become a catchphrase when someone encounters a difficulty. In fact, the official transcript shows that Lovell actually said, "Houston, we've had a problem." The filmmakers obviously thought this did not sound as good.

HISTORY DETECTIVES:
SKIMMING AND SCANNING

With very long documents, either online or in books, skimming can come in handy. When you skim, you do not read all the text word for word. Instead, you let your eyes skim over the text and look out for useful points, so that you get the overall sense. You can also scan the text, which means checking each page for key words or phrases.

▼ This is a scene from the movie *Apollo 13*, which was billed as a "riveting action-drama." From left to right are actor Bill Paxton as LM pilot Fred Haise, Tom Hanks as commander Jim Lovell, and Kevin Bacon as CM pilot Jack Swigert.

HISTORY DETECTIVES: BIBLIOGRAPHIES

Researchers consult many books during the course of a project, and they usually produce an organized list called a bibliography (from the ancient Greek word for "writing books"). The alphabetical list should include all sources used. As a rule, it includes the name of the author, title, publisher details, and year of publication. As an example, here is a bibliography of some books written by lunar astronauts. Many were written with other authors.

Aldrin, Buzz, and Ken Abraham. *Magnificent Desolation: The Long Journey Home from the Moon*. New York: Three Rivers Press, 2009.

Cernan, Eugene, and Don Davis. *The Last Man on the Moon*. New York: St. Martin's Press, 2000.

Duke, Charlie, and Dotty Duke. *Moonwalker*. Nashville, Tenn.: Nelson, 1990.

Irwin, James B., and William A. Emerson. *To Rule the Night: The Discovery Voyage of Astronaut Jim Irwin*. Nashville, Tenn.: Holman, 1973.

Mitchell, Edgar, and Dwight Williams. *The Way of the Explorer*. New York: Putnam's, 1996.

Schmitt, Harrison H. *Return to the Moon: Exploration, Enterprise, and Energy in the Human Settlement of Space*. New York: Springer, 2006.

Shepard, Alan, and Deke Slayton. *Moon Shot*. New York: Open Road, 2011.

Young, John W., and James R. Hansen. *Forever Young: A Life of Adventure in Air and Space*. Gainesville: University Press of Florida, 2012.

LUNAR ROVING VEHICLE

Six of the twelve moonwalkers also drove on the Moon. The last three Apollo missions included a lunar roving vehicle (LRV). The vehicle was lowered from the LM with pulleys, and components then folded out and locked in place automatically. The LRV was powered by electric motors. The *Apollo 17* vehicle traveled a total distance of 22.3 miles (35.9 kilometers), and it drove up to 4.7 miles (7.6 kilometers) away from the lunar module. The LRV was fitted with a TV camera, which could be remotely controlled from Earth. At the end of the mission, the LRV was parked a safe distance from the LM and its camera showed the ascent stage liftoff.

▼ James Irwin (eighth man on the Moon) loads up the *Apollo 15* lunar rover with equipment. This was the first vehicle to travel on the lunar surface, and it is still there today.

WHAT HAPPENED TO THE LUNAR MODULES AND ROVERS?

It would be interesting to find out what happened to all the extra Apollo parts that did not return to Earth. You could start by visiting a Wikipedia article called "List of man-made objects on the Moon" (see page 34 for notes on using Wikipedia). The list includes all the Apollo missions, and for many objects it gives a precise lunar location. As an example, the *Apollo 16* lunar rover is listed at Moon coordinates 8° 58° 12° S, 15° 30° 36° E, very near the descent stage of the lunar module, code-named Orion. But what about the *Apollo 16* LM ascent stage? No location is given, but a footnote leads us to a NASA page, which states that:

> *After docking with the CSM at 03:35:18 UT, the LM was jettisoned into lunar orbit at 20:54:12 UT on 24 April. Loss of altitude control on the LM made the planned impact near the Apollo 16 site impossible, so it was left in lunar orbit with an estimated life of 1 year.*

▼ This NASA image of the Moon shows the location of the six Apollo landing sites and of some of the equipment left behind.

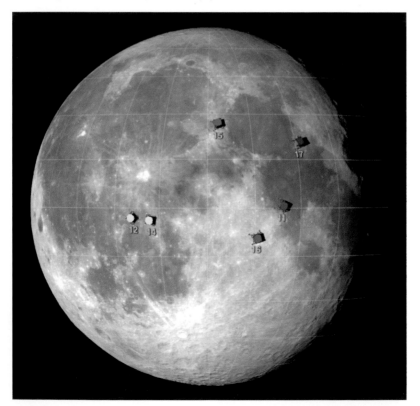

HISTORY DETECTIVES:
CONSULTING BOOKS

How do you know which books to look at to find out more about a subject? Any book you are interested in will probably include a description on the back cover. However, some will simply have reviews. Remember that these quotes are there to promote the book. There may be a more accurate description of the book in an introduction, in which the author or another expert tells the reader the purpose of the book and its general subject matter.

A Man on the Moon by Andrew Chaikin has a foreword by the actor Tom Hanks (star of *Apollo 13*), followed by the author's foreword, in which he describes his book as "the story of the lunar voyages that the astronauts never wrote." Online bookstores, such as Amazon, also give content notes on the books they sell. If you have the book in front of you, one way to get a quick overview is to look at the contents list (or table of contents), which often serves as an outline.

If you put "*Apollo 16* LM-11 (*Orion*) ascent stage" into a search engine, you should find a space.com site with a page called "Moon: space programs' dumping ground." This shows locations on a Moon map, including the 3rd-stage rocket (S-IVB) and LM descent stage for *Apollo 16*. But for the ascent stage, it states "Crashed (EOM)," standing for "end of mission." Seventy other human-made objects are listed. In the future, a location might be found for the remains of the *Apollo 16* lunar module. Do you think this is likely? You could do some research to find out.

WHO TRAINED TO GO TO THE MOON?

The 24 lunar astronauts would never have reached the Moon without the pioneering work of earlier men and women in the space program. The first man in space was a Russian **cosmonaut**, Yuri Gagarin, and U.S. astronaut Alan Shepard followed less than four weeks later, in 1961. Shepard was one of seven men in NASA's first group of astronauts, who had been selected in April 1959. The initial qualifications specified males between the ages of 25 and 40, less than 5 foot, 11 inches (1.8 meters) tall, with a bachelor's degree. The height restriction was there because of the limited size of the spacecraft. Three of the successful first group came from the U.S. Air Force, three from the Navy, and one from the Marines. There were two civilians in the second group of astronauts, including Neil Armstrong, who had previously been in the Air Force.

◀ Alan Shepard, in his space suit, heads toward the Redstone rocket that sent him into space on May 5, 1961, as part of the **Mercury** mission. Ten years later, Shepard became the fifth man on the Moon.

WHO IN HISTORY

ALAN B. SHEPARD, JR.
1923–1998
BORN: East Derry, New Hampshire

EDUCATION: Bachelor's degree, U.S. Naval Academy, 1944
EXPERIENCE: After service in the U.S. Navy during World War II (1939–1945), Shepard was a test pilot, an instructor, and an aircraft readiness officer. From 1959 to 1974, he worked for NASA. He later worked in business and was president of the Mercury Seven Foundation.
NASA EXPERIENCE: He was a member of Group 1 (Mercury astronauts) in 1959, and became the first American (and second human) in space, on May 5, 1961. He was commander of *Apollo 14*, making him the fifth man on the Moon.
TIME IN SPACE: 216 hours and 57 minutes; 9 hours and 21 minutes on the Moon

FUN ON THE MOON

Exhibit number 98-15805-5 at the National Air and Space Museum in Washington, D.C., is a "lunar golf club." This unusual piece of equipment is the head of a six-iron golf club attached to the handle of a scoop used to collect lunar samples. Alan Shepard used it to hit golf balls on the Moon on February 6, 1971. His spacesuit made the golf swing difficult, but Shepard claimed that his second one-handed drive sent the ball "miles and miles and miles" due to the low gravity on the Moon.

NASA ASTRONAUT GROUPS

Five groups of astronauts provided the 12 Apollo moonwalkers.

Group	Date	Nickname	Number of applicants	Number in group	Moonwalkers
1	1959	Mercury Seven	508	7	Shepard
2	1962	The Next Nine	250	9	Armstrong, Conrad, Young
3	1963	The Fourteen	400	14	Aldrin, Bean, Cernan, Scott
4	1965	The Scientists	1,500	6	Schmitt
5	1966	The Original Nineteen	351	19	Duke, Irwin, Mitchell

DID WOMEN TRAIN TO GO TO THE MOON?

Women did train to go to the Moon, and you can read all about them on the NASA web site. Thirteen women were known as First Lady Astronaut Trainees (FLATs), and the NASA piece below describes their training. As the extract from *Right Stuff, Wrong Sex* by Margaret A. Weitekamp points out (see the box on page 43), there were reasons why women never qualified to join the Apollo program. The first American woman in space was Sally Ride, who joined NASA in 1978 and five years later flew on the space shuttle *Challenger*.

THE WOMAN IN SPACE PROGRAM

Because, on the average, women are smaller and lighter than men are, scientists speculated that they might make good occupants for cramped space vehicles. In 1960, Dr. William Randolph "Randy" Lovelace II and Brig. General Donald Flickinger invited award-winning pilot Geraldyn "Jerrie" Cobb to undergo the physical testing regimen [program] that Lovelace's Albuquerque, New Mexico Foundation had developed to help select NASA's first astronauts... When Cobb became the first woman to pass those tests, Lovelace announced her success at a 1960 conference in Stockholm, Sweden...

The Lovelace doctors required very thorough examinations. These included numerous X-rays and a four-hour eye exam. A specially weighted stationary bicycle pushed the women to exhaustion while testing their respiration. The doctors had the women swallow a rubber tube so that they could test their stomach acids. A tilt table tested circulation. Using an electrical pulse, the physicians tested nerve reflexes in their arms. Ice water was shot into the women's ears to induce vertigo so that the doctors could time how quickly they recovered...

In the end, thirteen women passed the same physical examinations that the Lovelace Foundation had developed for NASA's astronaut selection process... A few days before they were to report [for further tests], however, the women received telegrams abruptly canceling the Pensacola testing.

Source: history.nasa.gov

⚠ The six manned Mercury missions between 1961 and 1963 were all piloted by men. Jerrie Cobb was an experienced pilot, but she never went into space. She became a NASA consultant in 1961.

MASCULINE ROLE?

Space policy makers…feared that any harm to a female astronaut would outrage a public that remained protective of women… The prospect of subjecting a woman to mortal danger betrayed the rigidly defined gender roles asserted in post-war America. Given the military background of the leaders of the new civilian American space agency, many NASA officials simply could not conceive of women in the masculine role of astronaut.

Source: *Right Stuff, Wrong Sex* by Margaret A. Weitekamp (Baltimore: Johns Hopkins University Press, 2004)

WHY NO WOMEN?

Why were there no women among the moonwalkers? Try looking for evidence of medical research or the results of the physical tests that astronauts had to undergo. One research study in 2001, by three medical experts (two women and a man) from the National Space Biomedical Research Institute and other research establishments, measured how lightheaded and faint astronauts felt after spaceflight. They found that 100 percent of the women but only 20 percent of the men had these symptoms. They were all recruited from the Astronaut Corps at Johnson Space Center and had flown on space shuttles, but there were far fewer female subjects (5) than male (30), so perhaps the figures are misleading. What do you think of the results? And have things changed much over time? Figures show that since 2000, 207 astronauts have visited the International Space Station, of whom 31 were women. That is just 15 percent. Do you think this is the right percentage? What evidence is your opinion based on?

▼ James McDivitt has his eyes tested in 1965. That year, he commanded *Gemini 4*, which made 66 Earth orbits on a four-day mission. McDivitt had been a brigadier general in the U.S. Air Force and flew 145 combat missions during the Korean War.

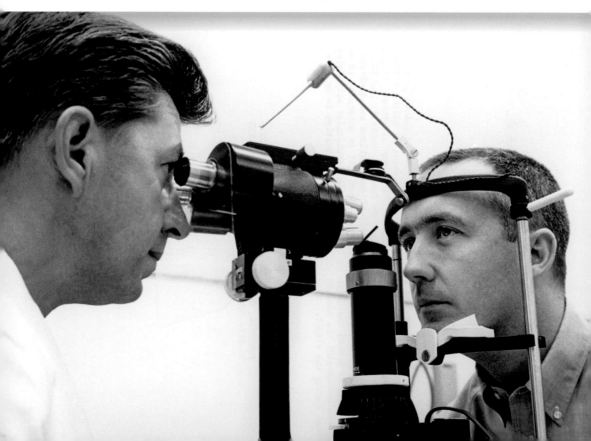

HISTORY DETECTIVES: TIMELINES

Dates are important in any study of history. Researchers often present these in a timeline, which helps them and others to see how developments fit together. The timeline can be a simple list of dates, such as the one below, or similar to the more comprehensive timeline on pages 58–59. It can be presented in a more graphic way, too, with dates and events spread across or down the page.

1959	NASA Group 1 recruited	1966	NASA Group 5 recruited
1960		1967	
1961		1968	*Apollo 7, Apollo 8*
1962	NASA Group 2 recruited	1969	*Apollo 9, Apollo 10, Apollo 11, Apollo 12*
1963	NASA Group 3 recruited		
1964		1970	*Apollo 13*
1965	NASA Group 4 recruited	1971	*Apollo 14, Apollo 15*
		1972	*Apollo 16, Apollo 17*

LEADING UP TO SUCCESS

This table shows the four most important Apollo missions leading up to the first lunar landing. The *Apollo 10* lunar module (code name *Snoopy*) came within 9¾ miles (15.6 kilometers) of the Moon's surface.

Apollo number	Rocket	Commander	Launch date	Achievement
7	*Saturn IB*	Wally Schirra	Oct. 11, 1968	CSM makes 163 Earth orbits
8	*Saturn V*	Frank Borman	Dec. 21, 1968	CSM makes 10 lunar orbits
9	*Saturn V*	James McDivitt	March 3, 1969	CSM docks with LM and makes 151 Earth orbits
10	*Saturn V*	Thomas Stafford	May 18, 1969	CSM and LM make 31 lunar orbits

HISTORIC MOMENTS

There were many historic events leading up to the first Moon landing. Two very important moments occurred during the *Apollo 8* mission in 1968, which was the first to take astronauts to the Moon. At 2 hours, 27 minutes, and 22 seconds after launch, the **capsule communicator (CapCom)** Michael Collins in Houston Mission Control told the spacecraft commander (SC) Frank Borman that they were "go for TLI." That meant that everything was ready for the first **trans-lunar injection**, a maneuver that turned them away from Earth and sent them on the way to the Moon. Later in the flight (at 69 hours, 51 minutes, 16 seconds), CM pilot James Lovell gave the first close-up description of the Moon as he told Mission Control, "Okay, Houston. The Moon is essentially gray, no color; looks like plaster of Paris or sort of a grayish beach sand."

```
APOLLO 8 MISSION COMMENTARY, 12/21/68, GET 22600, CST 9:17A  26/1

        PAO              This is Apollo Control Houston at 2 hours,
26 minutes into the flight.  We have just acquired by Carnarvon,
and here is how that conversation is going.
        CAPCOM           Apollo 8, Houston.
        SC               Go ahead Houston.
        CAPCOM           Alright, you are GO for TLI, over.
        SC               Roger, we understand we are GO for TLI.
        PAO              This is Apollo Control Houston, running
through an unusually quiet pass across Carnarvon with very
little more than establishing call signs.  Our orbital digitals,
which we are reading out from Australian sites, show that
present velocity is 25 569 feet per second, showing an
apogee of 105.5 nautical miles; and our translunar injection
burn will have the effect, here's that comm going up, let's
catch up with it.
        SC               The following.
        CAPCOM           Alright, we will have LOS in about
30 seconds and we will pick you up over ARIA 1 at 237 and 1/2.
        SC               Roger.
        PAO              Apollo Control back here.  The TLI burn
will add 10 500 feet per second, perhaps a foot or more per
second; but that is pretty close.  Ten thousand, five hundred feet
per second to the present 25 570.  The duration of the burn
will be slightly more than 5 minutes.  It will occur 2 hours,
and 50 minutes into the flight.  Now, a combination of stations
will be seeing it .  The ship Mercury will see it, parked
about a thousand miles south of Hawaii.  Hawaii should also
see it.  In a very few minutes, as the spacecraft starts
away from the earth, the big dish in Goldstone, Calif., will
acquire.  At 2 hours, 33 minutes into the flight, this is
Apollo Control Houston.

        END OF TAPE
```

▲ NASA's original transcript records the conversation with *Apollo 8* commander Frank Borman beginning at 2 hours and 26 minutes into the flight. There are hundreds of these transcripts available to view on NASA's web site.

LEARNING FROM TRAGEDY

Experts sometimes have to investigate tragic events in order to improve things for the future. This was the case with *Apollo 1*. On January 27, 1967, three astronauts were in the command module on top of a Saturn rocket at Cape Canaveral in Florida. Command Pilot Gus Grissom, Senior Pilot Edward White, and Pilot Roger Chaffee were going through a simulated (pretend) launch, getting ready for the real thing planned for a month later. Suddenly, disaster struck. The command module caught fire, and all three astronauts were killed. The first manned Apollo mission was held up for 20 months while a full investigation took place.

▲ The burned-out command module of *Apollo 1* was moved to a storage container after the investigation into the tragedy.

READING THE ORIGINAL REPORT

The original report of the *Apollo 1* disaster can be seen online at the NASA web site, at history.nasa.gov/Apollo204/as204report.html. When you look at this or any other document relating to the fire tragedy, you might find the mission called *Apollo* (or *Apollo-Saturn*) *204*, which was its original title. It was renamed *Apollo 1* later. The accident led to a number of recommendations in the report and to changes in future spacecraft, including:

- Wiring was covered with protective insulation.
- The cabin pressure and pure-oxygen levels were lowered for the launch and ascent phases of a mission.
- Flammable materials were replaced with nonflammable ones.
- Nylon spacesuits were replaced with fireproof fiberglass fabric.
- An outward-opening explosive hatch was installed.

These changes led to the success of the first manned flight during the following year and the Moon landing two years later.

WHAT DID THE LUNAR ASTRONAUTS ACHIEVE?

Before humans stepped onto the Moon's surface, no one could be absolutely certain what they would find. Scientists were already sure that the ancient astronomers who called the lunar plains *maria* (meaning "seas") were wrong and that the surface was dry. Other theories had suggested a thick layer of dust covered the surface, but unmanned probe landings showed that this was wrong. Neil Armstrong was able to confirm both these facts from personal experience as soon as he made his famous "small step." In fact, scientists all over the world learned a great deal from the astronauts' descriptions, as well as from their other discoveries. Armstrong and the other 23 lunar astronauts found out a great deal about Earth's satellite.

▼ The famous "Earthrise" photograph was taken from the *Apollo 8* command module at 10:40 a.m. (Houston time) on December 24, 1968.

VICTORY IN THE SPACE RACE

World Book encyclopedia sums up the Apollo missions' achievements by saying: "The Apollo expeditions achieved the goal of demonstrating U.S. technological superiority, and the race to the moon ended with a clear-cut U.S. triumph." This "technological superiority" included developments in microelectronics (the design and use of microchips and computers), medical monitoring equipment, and scientific information about the makeup and origin of the Moon.

LEARNING ABOUT THE UNIVERSE

The astronauts learned a great deal about our solar system and the whole universe. They knew that what they were attempting was very dangerous, because they were exploring the unknown. Radiation might affect them badly, for example. Or they might come into contact with harmful substances, including **microorganisms**, that are not even known on Earth. But perhaps they did not expect to learn so much about their own home planet. Images such as the famous Earthrise photograph (opposite) made people realize how beautiful and vulnerable Earth is. Bill Anders, the astronaut who took the photograph, said, "We came all this way to explore the Moon, and the most important thing is that we discovered the Earth."

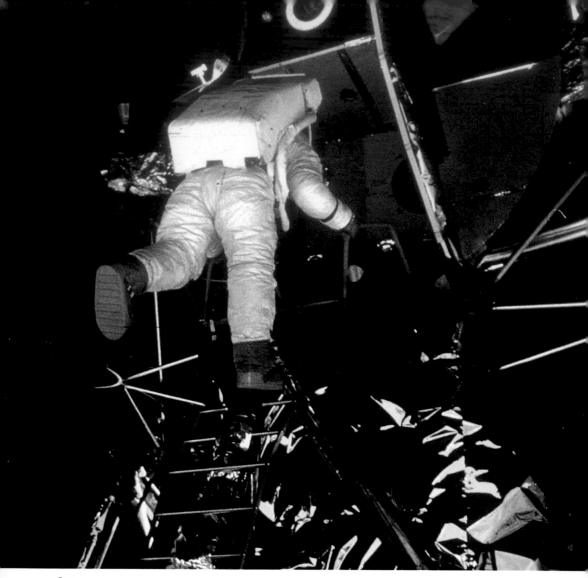

▲ Buzz Aldrin comes down *Eagle's* ladder before taking his first step on the Moon.

"MAGNIFICENT DESOLATION"

The first thing most of the 12 landing lunar astronauts did was to describe what they saw around them. NASA's Lunar Surface Journal records the following words between the first two men on the Moon when Buzz Aldrin emerged from the lunar module:

> *109:43:16 Aldrin: Beautiful view!*
> *109:43:18 Armstrong: Isn't that something! Magnificent sight out here.*
> *109:43:24 Aldrin: Magnificent desolation.*

Aldrin's two words of description became famous.

RESEARCHING ALDRIN'S WORDS

Author Andrew Chaikin wrote about this incident in his book *A Man on the Moon*. This is how he describes Aldrin's words and the situation leading up to them:

> Turning away, Armstrong began to dig into the surface, and what he found surprised him. Everywhere there was the same soft powder, and yet here and there he met resistance. He managed to scoop up enough dust to fill the bag, and even managed to snare a couple of small rocks; the **geologists**, he told himself, would get their money's worth. "That looks beautiful from here, Neil," Aldrin said. He was talking about the sample, but Armstrong responded as if he had meant the moon. "It has a stark beauty all its own," he said, excitement finally invading his voice. It was beautiful… There must be some combination of words that would describe it, but Aldrin could only utter, "Beautiful view!" Armstrong agreed. "Isn't that something? Magnificent sight out here." Hearing this, Aldrin suddenly had the words he was looking for. With quiet wonder in his voice, he said, "Magnificent desolation." Holding the ladder in both hands, Aldrin swung both feet out of the footpad and onto the moon.

Source: *A Man on the Moon* by Andrew Chaikin (New York: Viking Penguin, 1994)

IN ALDRIN'S OWN WORDS

Andrew Chaikin thought there was "quiet wonder" in Buzz Aldrin's voice. But what did Aldrin himself feel? If you do an Internet search for "magnificent desolation," you will find that Buzz Aldrin used these words as the title of a book he wrote, in which he said:

> In every direction I could see detailed characteristics of the gray ash-colored lunar scenery, pocked with thousands of little craters and with every variety and shape of rock. I saw the horizon curving a mile and a half away… I slowly allowed my eyes to drink in the unusual majesty of the moon. In its starkness and monochromatic hues, it was indeed beautiful. But it was a different sort of beauty than I had ever before seen. Magnificent, I thought, then said, "Magnificent desolation."

Source: *Magnificent Desolation* by Buzz Aldrin (New York: Three Rivers Press, 2009)

TOP TEN SCIENTIFIC DISCOVERIES

According to NASA, the Apollo program's top findings were as follows. Some of the discoveries were complex, but they are all very important to scientists. The finding that got the most coverage in the general press was number 5. There had always been the possibility that microscopic organisms might be found in Moon rocks.

1. The Moon has not existed from the beginning of time; it has internal layers similar to Earth.
2. The Moon is ancient and still preserves an early history (the first billion years) that must be common to all Earth-like planets.
3. The oldest Moon rocks are about 4.5 billion years old.
4. The Moon and Earth are related and formed from different proportions of the same materials.
5. The Moon is lifeless; it contains no living organisms, **fossils**, or organic compounds.
6. All Moon rocks originated through high-temperature processes with little or no involvement with water.
7. Early in its history, the Moon was made of hot, molten rocks.
8. The lunar ocean of molten rocks was followed by a series of huge **asteroid** impacts that created craters later filled by lava flows.
9. The Moon is not perfectly round, possibly because of the effect of Earth's gravity.
10. The surface of the Moon is covered by a rubble of rock fragments and dust, called the lunar regolith, that contains a radiation history of the Sun that could help us understand climate changes on Earth.

◀ *Apollo 12* LM pilot Alan Bean (the fourth man on the Moon) holds a sample container filled with lunar soil. Pete Conrad, who took the photograph, is reflected in Bean's visor.

HISTORY DETECTIVES:
INTERPRETING IMAGES

All U.S. lunar mission photographs come from NASA, and many are also available through commercial picture libraries. Very often, library captions are brief and uninformative. You must always ask yourself exactly what it is that you are looking at. The NASA caption to the photo below includes, "The rod to hold the flag out horizontally would not extend fully, so the flag ended up with a slight waviness, giving the appearance of being windblown. The flag itself was difficult to erect, it was very hard to penetrate beyond about 6 to 8 inches [15–20 centimeters] into the lunar soil with the flagstaff." This is useful information. It is probably there because there were suggestions by doubters that the photos had been faked, as there is no wind on the Moon, so the flag should have hung still. In fact, NASA had designed the flag to be held out.

▼ Buzz Aldrin stands beside the U.S. flag, which has a rod at the top so it appears to "fly."

LUNAR SAMPLES

Harrison Schmitt of *Apollo 17* was the only scientist among the lunar astronauts. He and Eugene Cernan collected the most lunar samples of any mission—249 pounds (115 kilograms). Altogether, the 12 moonwalkers collected 2,196 samples of rocks and soil, weighing a total of 842 pounds (382 kilograms). These were broken down into more than 110,000 individually catalogued samples. Many samples now appear in museums around the world.

One rock collected by Schmitt, "lunar basalt 70017," was later called the "Goodwill Rock." On Earth, it was broken into small fragments that were attached to wooden plaques and presented by President Nixon to all the countries of the world, as well as the individual U.S. states and territories.

▼ This sample, known as "Genesis Rock," was collected by *Apollo 15* astronauts Scott and Irwin. It is 4 billion years old and once floated on an ocean of molten rocks.

TRACKING DOWN MISSING ROCKS

Many of the Goodwill Rock fragments have since gone missing. Were they lost or stolen? In 1998, a former NASA special agent, Joseph Gutheinz, set up Operation Lunar Eclipse, placing advertisements in newspapers asking to buy moon rocks. He was soon offered one of the rocks, which had originally been presented to the nation of Honduras, for $5 million. He did not pay the money, but the seller was caught and the rock recovered. He found that other rocks had been offered for sale, one of them online in California. Gutheinz then set up a Moon Rock Recovery Project at the University of Phoenix, where he is a teacher. He asked his students to help him track down missing rocks, and they have so far succeeded with 78 samples. Many of the others are probably in private collections around the world.

SUCCESS IN ALASKA

In 2010, one of Joseph Gutheinz's students, Elizabeth Riker, started searching for five missing fragments of moon rock collected by *Apollo 11* and presented to the state of Alaska. The rock and its plaque had disappeared following a fire at the Transportation Museum in Anchorage in 1973, and efforts to trace it had come to a dead end. Riker searched through records and documents. Although she failed to trace the rock, she published her findings in an Alaskan newspaper. This led to a reader declaring that he had rescued the plaque from the fire and claiming ownership. The Alaska State Museum challenged the claim, and while this was being settled, the plaque was given to NASA for safekeeping. The museum finally won the right to exhibit the rock fragments again in December 2012.

▲ *Apollo 12* astronaut Pete Conrad (the third man on the Moon) inspects *Surveyor 3* before removing some parts. In the background at the top of the hill is lunar module *Intrepid,* which purposely landed in the Oceans of Storms near the probe.

INVESTIGATING *APOLLO 12* BACTERIA

One of the main reasons for collecting and studying lunar samples was to find out whether there was or ever had been life on the Moon. However, investigators also had to double check some of the findings. On November 19, 1969, *Apollo 12* astronauts Pete Conrad and Alan Bean landed on the lunar surface within walking distance of the unmanned *Surveyor 3* probe, which had landed two years earlier. They removed the probe's camera and brought it back to Earth. The camera was found to contain bacteria. Could this living material have come from the Moon? Research scientists decided that the bacteria had probably gotten on to the camera on Earth before it was ever launched.

In 2011, after a long period of further research, three scientists published their findings on the bacteria in a paper called *Microbes on the Moon?* They decided that the bacteria had in fact been transferred to the camera from the scientists studying it after its return to Earth. They recommended that in the future, all studies on Earth must be made in completely sterile conditions. The astronauts themselves had always gone straight into quarantine after returning home.

HISTORY DETECTIVES: HANDS-ON RESEARCH

You can do your own practical research by visiting museums and looking at lunar exhibits. You will find a list of worldwide locations of the Goodwill Rocks at collectspace.com. You can find the current locations of the Apollo command modules at nssdc.gsfc.nasa.gov. The *Apollo 11* LM *Columbia* is at the Smithsonian National Air and Space Museum, in Washington, D.C., along with many other Apollo items. They include items such as Michael Collins's sunglasses, the Surveyor 3 camera, and a "urine collection and transfer hose" used by the astronauts.

IN THEIR OWN WORDS

Today, many former astronauts have their own web site. The "last man on the Moon," Eugene Cernan, believes that others will follow in his footsteps and add to the number who have been to the Moon. He writes at genecernan.com:

> *Too many years have passed for me to still be the last man to have left his footprints on the Moon. I believe with all my heart that somewhere out there is a young boy or girl with indomitable will and courage who will lift that dubious distinction from my shoulders and take us back where we belong. Let us give that dream a chance.*

TIMELINE

| 1960 | **Jan. 18**: President Dwight D. Eisenhower approves the Saturn rocket project |
| | **July 28**: Announcement of Project Apollo |

1961	**April 12**: Soviet Yuri Gagarin is the first person in space
	May 5: Alan Shepard is the first American in space
	May 25: President John F. Kennedy announces the goal of landing astronauts on the Moon before 1970
	Oct. 27: Launch of the first successful Saturn rocket

| 1962 | **Feb. 20**: John Glenn is the first American to orbit Earth |
| | **July 11**: NASA announces lunar orbit rendezvous as the system for sending astronauts to the Moon |

| 1963 | **June 16**: Soviet Valentina Tereshkova is the first woman in space |

| 1965 | **March 18**: Soviet Alexei Leonov is the first EVA spacewalker |
| | **June 3**: Edward White is the first American spacewalker |

| 1966 | **Jan. 31**: Soviet unmanned spacecraft *Luna 9* makes the first soft landing on the Moon |
| | **June 2**: *Surveyor 1* is the first U.S. spacecraft to make a soft landing on the Moon |

| 1967 | **Jan. 27**: *Apollo 1* astronauts Chaffee, Grissom, and White are killed during a ground test |
| | **Nov. 9**: An unmanned *Apollo 4* command module launches on a *Saturn V* rocket |

1968	**Jan. 22**: *Apollo 5* launches with the first lunar module
	Sept. 14: Soviet spacecraft *Zond 5* carries tortoises, worms, and flies around the Moon and back to Earth
	Oct. 11: *Apollo 7* launches astronauts into Earth's orbit
	Dec. 24: *Apollo 8* crew are the first humans to orbit the Moon

1969   **March 7**: Apollo 9 lunar module Spider separates from
command module Gumdrop in a successful test in Earth's orbit
May 22: Apollo 10 lunar module Snoopy approaches the lunar
surface, as a rehearsal for landing
July 20: Apollo 11 lunar module Eagle lands on the Moon at the
Sea of Tranquility and stays for 22 hours (with a moonwalk of
2 hours, 30 minutes)
Nov. 19: Apollo 12 lunar module Intrepid lands on the Moon
at the Ocean of Storms and stays for 1 day and 8 hours (with
moonwalks of 7 hours, 45 minutes)

1970   **Jan. 4**: Apollo 20 (scheduled for December 1972) is canceled,
so the launch vehicle can be used for the Skylab space station
April 14: An explosion aboard Apollo 13 forces the astronauts
to return to Earth
Sept. 2: Apollo 18 (scheduled for February 1972) and Apollo 19
(scheduled for July 1972) are canceled
Nov. 10: Soviet Luna 17 unmanned probe deploys the lunar
roving vehicle Lunokhod 1

1971   **Feb. 5**: Apollo 14 lunar module Antares lands on the
Moon at Fra Mauro and stays for 1 day and 10
hours (with moonwalks of 9 hours, 21 minutes)
July 30: Apollo 15 lunar module Falcon lands on the Moon at
Hadley-Apennine and stays for 2 days and 19 hours (with
moonwalks of 18 hours and 33 minutes)

1972   **Feb. 14**: Soviet Luna 20 unmanned probe collects lunar
samples and returns them to Earth
April 20: Apollo 16 lunar module Orion lands on the Moon at
Descartes Highlands and stays for 2 days and 23 hours (with
moonwalks of 20 hours and 14 minutes)
Dec. 11: Apollo 17 lunar module Challenger lands on the
Moon at Taurus-Littrow and stays for 3 days and 3 hours
(with moonwalks of 22 hours and 2 minutes)

GLOSSARY

abort bring something to an end because of a problem

aeronautical engineering science of design and construction of aircraft and spacecraft

ascent stage upper part of the lunar module that took the astronauts back from the Moon to the command module

asteroid rock orbiting the Sun

astronautics science of space exploration

capsule communicator (CapCom) person in Mission Control who speaks to astronauts in space

command module (CM) part of a spacecraft that carries astronauts into space and back; the Apollo CM orbited the Moon without landing

command/service module (CSM) command and service modules linked together

cosmonaut Russian astronaut

descent stage lower part of the lunar module that stayed on the Moon

dock join two spacecraft together

eject escape from a craft by being thrown out at great speed

extravehicular activity (EVA) astronauts' activity outside a spacecraft; spacewalk or moonwalk

flight simulator machine for training pilots on the ground that acts like a spacecraft in flight

fossil remains of a prehistoric animal or plant

Gemini second series of U.S. human spaceflight missions, after Mercury (1962–1966)

geologist scientist who studies the structure of Earth or the Moon

gigabyte unit of computer memory or data (billion bytes)

gravity force that attracts things toward the center of Earth or another planet or star

hyperlink link that works by clicking on a highlighted word or image

industrial archaeology study of past industrial equipment and buildings

interactive with a two-way flow of information between a user and a computer

kilobyte unit of computer memory or data (thousand bytes)

lunar module (LM) part of a spacecraft that lands on the Moon

lunar orbit circling the Moon

Lunar Reconnaissance Orbiter (LRO) unmanned U.S. spacecraft launched in 2009 to orbit the Moon and map its surface

lunar-orbit rendezvous (LOR) system of a separate module landing on the Moon before returning to the main spacecraft

maneuver movement requiring skill and care

Mercury first series of U.S. human spaceflight missions (1959–1963)

meteorologist weather expert

microorganism microscopic living thing, such as a bacterium or virus

Mission Control building in Houston, Texas, where experts controlled Apollo space flights

moonquake tremor of the Moon's surface

payload weight of spacecraft and equipment carried by a rocket

propellant rocket fuel

quarantine period when astronauts are kept in isolation to prevent them from catching or spreading disease

rocketry science of rockets

seismometer instrument that measures the force of earthquakes and moonquakes

service module (SM) part of a spacecraft that carries fuel and supplies

sonar system for detecting underwater objects using sound pulses and their echoes

thrust force of a rocket engine

trans-lunar injection (TLI) procedure to send a spacecraft from Earth's orbit toward the Moon

waveform shape of a sound wave

waxing crescent Moon the Moon appearing to increase in size day by day as seen from Earth

FIND OUT MORE

BOOKS

Chaikin, Andrew. *A Man on the Moon: The Voyages of the Apollo Astronauts*. New York: Penguin, 2007.

Couper, Heather, and Nigel Henbest. *Encyclopedia of Space*. New York: Dorling Kindersley, 2003.

Oxlade, Chris, and David West. *The Apollo Missions and Other Adventures in Space*. New York: Rosen, 2012.

Pyle, Rod. *Destination Moon: The Apollo Missions in the Astronauts' Own Words*. New York: HarperCollins, 2005.

WEB SITE

www.nasa.gov

This is the site of the U.S. National Aeronautics and Space Administration (NASA).

MOVIES

Apollo 13, directed by Ron Howard (Universal Pictures, 1995): This docudrama tells the story of the mission that had to be cut short.

Moonwalk One, directed by Theo Kamecke (1970; Quality Information Publishers, 2007): This documentary is about *Apollo 11*.

PLACES TO VISIT

Smithsonian National Air and Space Museum

Independence Avenue at 6th Street, SW
Washington, D.C. 20560
airandspace.si.edu

Space Center Houston

1601 NASA Parkway
Houston, Texas 77058
spacecenter.org

OTHER TOPICS TO RESEARCH

There are many different topics related to the astronauts who went to the Moon. Here are some more research ideas.

Where were you?

Several web sites carry stories about what people remember about July 20, 1969, and especially where they were when the *Eagle* landed. This could make a good research project. You could interview your grandparents and their friends and record their memories. It would be easiest to use a recorder and type their words up later on your computer. This piece of oral history will be a primary source in the sense that your interviewees will be saying what happened at the time. If you want to, you could submit your story to the web site wherewereyou.com.

What if?

This book starts with the *Eagle* landing. The reason Neil Armstrong risked running so low on fuel was because he was looking for a flat landing place, without boulders or craters. If the lunar module had landed and toppled, it could have never taken off again. Armstrong had dealt skillfully with an emergency on *Gemini 8* three years earlier. He was clearly an amazing astronaut. What do you think would have happened to the Moon program if *Apollo 11* had failed?

Politicians had thought about what to do if Armstrong and Aldrin got stranded on the Moon. President Nixon had a speech prepared, which began: "Fate has ordained that the men who went to the moon to explore in peace will stay on the moon to rest in peace." You can read the whole speech at space.com and other web sites. Put the first sentence into a search engine to locate the speech.

One small step for [a] man...

You could research when Neil Armstrong thought these words up. He said that the historic words were unplanned, but in a documentary in 2012, Neil's brother Dean said he showed him a written version of the speech months before the *Apollo 11* launch.

INDEX

Aldrin, Buzz 4, 6, 7, 8, 9, 10–11, 20, 22, 23, 25, 26, 31, 50, 51, 53
Anders, Bill 12, 13, 49
Apollo 1 disaster 47
Apollo 11 mission 4–5, 6, 7, 8–9, 14–16, 18, 20–28
Apollo 13 mission 12, 32, 34–35
Apollo missions' achievements 48–49, 52
Armstrong, Neil 4, 6, 7, 8, 9, 10, 20, 21, 22, 23, 24, 25, 31, 40, 48, 50, 51
artworks on the Moon 33

backup crews 12–13
Bean, Alan 31, 33, 52, 56
Bezos, Jeff 18
blastoff 15

Cernan, Eugene 31, 54, 57
Cobb, Jerrie 42, 43
Cold War 28
Collins, Michael 6, 7, 8, 10, 11, 13, 25, 32
command modules 6, 14, 15, 24, 34, 47
command/service module (CSM) 14, 15, 33
computers 24, 49
Conrad, Pete 31, 52, 56
conspiracy theorists 16

declassified documents 29
descriptions of the Moon 46, 50–51
docking 7, 11
Duke, Charles 30, 31

Eagle 4, 20, 21, 25, 26, 50
"Earthrise" photograph 48, 49
environmental movement 49
extravehicular activity (EVA) 8, 30

famous words 4, 24, 35
fighter pilots 7, 8, 10
flight simulators 9
"flying bedstead" 9

Gagarin, Yuri 40
Gemini missions 7, 8, 10, 12, 31, 32, 44
golf, lunar 41
Goodwill Rocks 54–55, 57

Haise, Fred 12, 13, 32
human interest stories 26

Irwin, James 31, 37

Kennedy, John F. 5

landing sites 38
life on the Moon 56–57
Lovell, Jim 12, 13, 32, 35, 46
low fuel problem 21
lunar modules 4, 8–9, 14, 15, 20, 21, 23, 24, 25, 30, 34, 38–39
lunar roving vehicle (LRV) 37
Lunar Surface Journal 21, 24, 50
lunar-orbit rendezvous 14

man-made objects on the Moon 38–39
Mission Control, Houston 4, 15, 20, 29
mission times 15
Mitchell, Edgar 31
Moon landing, first 4–5, 20–27

NASA 6, 8, 10, 16, 18, 23, 26, 40, 46
Nixon, Richard 23, 29, 54

problems 21, 34–35

quarantine 13, 28, 29, 57

research 6
bibliographies 36
biographies 13
books and films 6, 13, 22, 35, 36, 39, 51
inaccurate information 27
industrial archaeology 18
Internet research 19, 23, 24, 34, 38–39
museums 41, 57
photographs 53
primary sources 11
secondary sources 22
skimming and scanning 35
timelines 34, 45, 58–59
Wikipedia 34, 38
Ride, Sally 42

Saturn V rockets 14, 15, 16–17, 19
Schmitt, Harrison 31, 54
scientific discoveries 52
Scott, David 31
service modules 14
Shepard, Alan 31, 40, 41
soil and rock samples 23, 51, 52, 54–55
Soviet Union 28, 40
"space race" 28
splashdown 28–29

technological developments 49
test pilots 7, 10
tragic events 47
training 8–9, 11, 12
trans-lunar injection 46

videotapes, missing 26

women astronauts 42–44

Young, John 30, 31